BIRDS

A to Z

A FIREFLY BOOK

Published by Firefly Books Ltd. 2009

First printing

Publisher Cataloging-in-Publication Data (U.S.)

Earley, Chris G.
         Birds A to Z / Chris G. Earley / photographs by Robert McCaw.
[32] p. : col. photos. ; cm.
Summary: Description of twenty-six birds, including Latin name, diet, range, length, weight, wingspan and nest.
ISBN-13: 978-1-55407-554-6 (bound)   ISBN-10: 1-55407-554-8 (bound)
ISBN-13: 978-1-55407-500-3 (pbk.)   ISBN-10: 1-55407-500-9 (pbk.)
1. Birds—Juvenile literature. I. McCaw, Robert. II. Title.

Library and Archives Canada Cataloguing in Publication

Earley, Chris G, 1968–
         Birds A to Z / Chris Earley ; Robert McCaw, photographs.
ISBN-13: 978-1-55407-554-6 (bound)   ISBN-10: 1-55407-554-8 (bound)
ISBN-13: 978-1-55407-500-3 (pbk.)   ISBN-10: 1-55407-500-9 (pbk.)
    1. Birds—Juvenile literature. 2. Birds—Identification—Juvenile literature. 3. Birds—Pictorial works—Juvenile literature.
I. McCaw, Robert II. Title.
QL676.2.E28 2009   j598   C2009-901363-0

Published in the United States by
Firefly Books (U.S.) Inc.
P.O. Box 1338, Ellicott Station
Buffalo, New York 14205

Published in Canada by
Firefly Books Ltd.
66 Leek Crescent
Richmond Hill, Ontario L4B 1H1

Cover and Interior Design: Erin R. Holmes/Soplari Design

Printed in China

The publisher gratefully acknowledges the financial support for our publishing program by the Government of Canada through the Book Publishing Industry Development Program.

BIRDS
A to Z

Chris G. Earley
Photographs by Robert McCaw

FIREFLY BOOKS

INTRODUCTION

Birds are cool. The variety of shapes, colors and sizes of birds makes them stand out. And the fact that most of them can fly causes us to be in awe of these feathered wonders. This book features a few of the over 10,000 species of birds that share this planet with us. It is hoped that these pages will inspire you to watch the birds in your own neighborhood and to connect with the natural world.

Chris Earley and Robert McCaw

ACKNOWLEDGMENTS

Thanks goes to all of the folks at Firefly Books for their friendly input and patience in looking after all the details in creating this book. A special thanks goes to Erin Holmes for her ability to take Robert's bird pictures and Chris' words and create a beautiful design for each and every page.

Thanks also to Glen Tepke for providing images of Xantus's Murrelet for the letter "X" and Brian Small for his Zone-Tailed Hawk photos for "Z." And thank you to Jiffy Gibson and Nathan Earley for reviewing earlier drafts of this book.

It is always a pleasure to spend time outdoors, and especially with the main characters of this book, the wild birds themselves. We need to thank them all for allowing us to watch them, take their picture, and to wish that they will always be there as part of our shared natural world.

DEDICATION

To my Grandchildren … May they have a keen desire to learn about nature and come to appreciate and respect all wild creatures that share the world with us.

Robert McCaw

To Mitchell, Rylie, Dougie, Colin and Frankie. Love, Uncle Chris

Contents

ANHINGA

A "Anhinga" is a South American Tupi word meaning "water turkey." It has a long neck and tail like a turkey, but unlike the Thanksgiving bird, the Anhinga is a really good swimmer and is great at fishing. It uses its sharp beak and long neck to spear fish. It even has sawlike edges on its beak that work like teeth to help it hold on to its slippery prey. To get close to its next meal, the Anhinga acts like a stealthy submarine. It often moves around underwater with only its head and neck sticking out above the surface, just like a periscope. This makes it look a bit like a snake and gives it one of its other names: Snakebird. When it is done swimming and hunting, the Anhinga often perches in the sunlight with its wings spread out. This helps it warm up after being in the water for so long and gives its wet feathers a chance to dry out.

ANHINGA

LATIN NAME	*Anhinga anhinga*
LENGTH	35" (89 cm)
WINGSPAN	45" (114 cm)
WEIGHT	2.7 lb (1.2 kg)
DIET	Mainly fish, some other aquatic animals
RANGE	Extreme southeastern U.S. to Brazil
NESTING SITE	In branches of trees or shrubs 3–98 ft (1–30 m) over water

EASTERN BLUEBIRD

LATIN NAME	*Sialia sialis*
LENGTH	7" (18 cm)
WINGSPAN	13" (33 cm)
WEIGHT	1.1 oz (31g)
DIET	Insects, some berries and fruits
RANGE	Southcentral and southeastern Canada to Nicaragua
NESTING SITE	Old woodpecker hole, natural cavity or nest box

Mountain Bluebird

BLUEBIRD

Twenty years ago, Eastern Bluebirds were considered rare in many parts of eastern Canada. This once common bird may have declined in numbers for many reasons, one being the loss of nesting sites. Bluebirds nest in old woodpecker holes in dead trees. In many areas, we removed dead trees and this has left fewer for the woodpeckers and then for the bluebirds. As well, introduced European Starlings and House Sparrows from Europe competed for the holes with the bluebirds. Naturalists then came to the rescue by building nest boxes that look like natural holes to a home-hunting bluebird. Now Eastern Bluebirds are becoming common once again. Other bluebird species as well as some warblers, flycatchers, swallows, wrens and chickadees also use nest boxes. Try putting some nest boxes in your backyard, schoolyard or local park and see what birds you can attract.

CHICKADEE

Most people know the bird that calls out its name with a loud "chick-a-dee-dee-dee!" Chickadees commonly visit backyard bird feeders across much of North America. These little birds are often quite bold and can become very used to people. If you hold out a handful of sunflower seeds, you may entice a local chickadee to land on your fingers. After it flies off with a seed in its beak, it might stop nearby, transfer its prize to its feet and then peck the seed open and eat it. But it may decide to store the seed somewhere instead. One Black-capped Chickadee may hide almost 1000 seeds in one day! What is even more amazing is the fact that it can remember where they are all hidden. Storing food and remembering where it is helps chickadees have enough to eat through the cold winter months.

Chestnut-backed Chickadee

BLACK-CAPPED CHICKADEE

LATIN NAME	*Poecile atricapillus*
LENGTH	5.25" (13 cm)
WINGSPAN	8" (20 cm)
WEIGHT	.39 oz (11g)
DIET	Insects, spiders, seeds and berries
RANGE	Alaska to Newfoundland and south to the central U.S.
NESTING SITE	Self-made cavity in rotting wood or an old woodpecker hole, natural cavity or nest box

D DUCK

There are over 30 different kinds of ducks that can be found in North America. Beginning bird-watchers often start with ducks because the males are fairly easy to identify. One of the first questions to ask yourself when you see a duck is whether it is a dabbler or a diver. When in the water, dabbling ducks, such as the Mallard, usually feed on the surface or dunk the front half of their bodies underwater while their bottoms stick out above the surface. Diving ducks, like the Common Goldeneye, usually feed by diving completely under the water. This allows them to eat underwater plants, crayfish, clams and fish, depending on the species of duck. The Wood Duck employs its own special feeding strategy. It not only dabbles like other ducks, but it will often eat acorns it finds while waddling around in forested areas.

Common Goldeneye

WOOD DUCK

LATIN NAME	*Aix sponsa*
LENGTH	18.5" (45 cm)
WINGSPAN	30" (76 cm)
WEIGHT	11 oz (300 g)
DIET	Seeds, fruits, insects and small aquatic animals
RANGE	Southern Canada, the U.S. and Cuba
NESTING SITE	Old woodpecker hole, natural cavity or nest box

Snowy Egret

EGRET

Egrets are elegant-looking herons. Their pure white plumage, long legs and long necks are very attractive, especially to other egrets. During the breeding season they expand their beauty by sporting long, wispy feathers called aigrettes. Unfortunately for the egrets, humans find these special feathers just as beautiful as their potential mates do. In the late 1800s and early 1900s, hundreds of thousands of egrets were killed so that their aigrettes could be put on ladies' hats. In 1903, the plumes sold for up to $32 per ounce, which was twice the value of gold at that time! Naturalist groups did their best to try to educate the public about the excessive killing of egrets and many other species of birds for their feathers. It wasn't until the 1910s that the fashion of wearing feathers had dwindled and egret populations were allowed to take the slow road to recovery. Many egret species are now common once more.

GREAT EGRET

LATIN NAME	*Ardea alba*
LENGTH	39" (99 cm)
WINGSPAN	51" (130 cm)
WEIGHT	1.9 lb (870 g)
DIET	Mainly fish, some insects, crustaceans, amphibians and even small birds and mammals
RANGE	Extreme southern Canada to southern Chile, southern Europe, Asia, Africa, Australia and New Zealand
NESTING SITE	Usually in trees up to 90 ft (27 m); sometimes on the ground

F FALCON

The Peregrine Falcon is the fastest animal on Earth. When it is diving for its avian prey, this speedy bird can go over 200 miles per hour (320 km/h). That's over three times as fast as most cars are going on the highway! The Peregrine gets to this incredible speed by flying high and then turning headfirst toward the ground and tucking in its long, pointed wings. This gives it a very streamlined shape. This powerful predator is going so fast that its prey is sometimes killed instantly by the impact of the falcon's talons. Another quick member of the falcon family is the much smaller Merlin. It often perches and waits for a small bird to fly across an open area such as a lake, field or beach. The Merlin then takes off and chases its prey down with a very fast, flapping flight. The American Kestrel is a less-speedy falcon. This bird hunts its insect, bird and small mammal prey from a perch or while hovering into the wind. The American Kestrel is the smallest falcon in North America and is also the most colorful raptor in the world.

PEREGRINE FALCON

LATIN NAME	Falco peregrinus
LENGTH	16" (41 cm)
WINGSPAN	41" (104 cm)
WEIGHT	1.6 lb (720 g)
DIET	Mostly birds, from small songbirds to small geese; some bats and rodents
RANGE	Worldwide, from Greenland to Tasmania
NESTING SITE	On cliffs, buildings, bridges, old raven and raptor stick nests

American Kestrel

GALLINULE

Another of North America's colorful birds is the eye-catching Purple Gallinule of the rail family. It is found in the southernmost areas of the eastern United States. It is here that this gorgeous bird has a bit of a problem with its neighbors. The wetlands that it lives in are often the home of alligators. The gallinule avoids alligators by having very long toes. These special toes help spread out the bird's body weight, allowing it to run along on top of floating lily pads as it looks for food. This helps it stay away from alligators much of the time. Unfortunately, alligators still sometimes eat the eggs in the gallinule's nest. However, alligators aren't all bad. Their presence may stop other nest predators from swimming to the islands and floating mats of vegetation that the gallinules nest on.

PURPLE GALLINULE

LATIN NAME	*Gallinula chloropus*
LENGTH	13" (33 cm)
WINGSPAN	22" (56 cm)
WEIGHT	11 oz (315 g)
DIET	Seeds, flowers, fruits, insects, crustaceans, worms and mollusks
RANGE	Southeastern U.S. (Gulf states) to northern Argentina
NESTING SITE	On floating mats of vegetation or in tall water plants

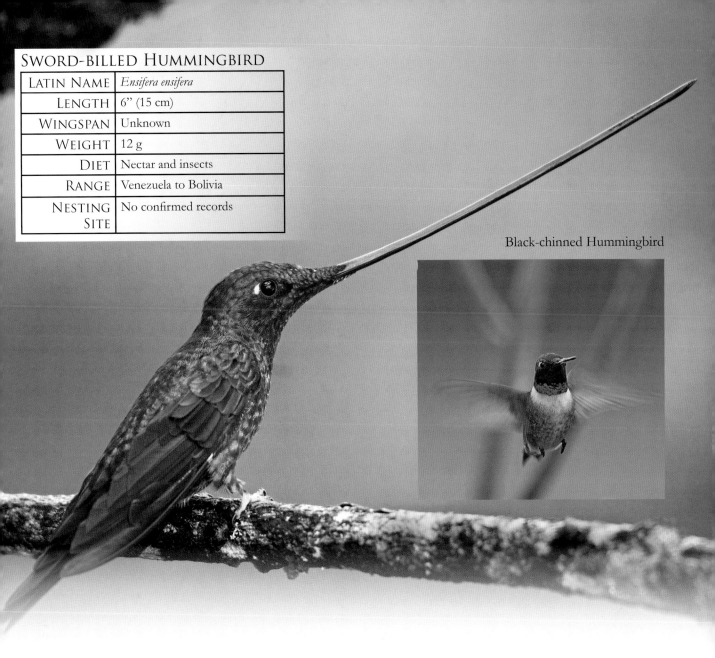

SWORD-BILLED HUMMINGBIRD

LATIN NAME	*Ensifera ensifera*
LENGTH	6" (15 cm)
WINGSPAN	Unknown
WEIGHT	12 g
DIET	Nectar and insects
RANGE	Venezuela to Bolivia
NESTING SITE	No confirmed records

Black-chinned Hummingbird

HUMMINGBIRD

There are so many incredible facts about hummingbirds that it is hard to know where to begin. They are the world's smallest birds. The smallest hummingbird weighs about the same as a penny and the biggest weighs three times that. There are over 320 species of hummingbirds and they are only found in North and South America. They can hover and fly backwards; these aerial exploits are possible because they can beat their wings up to 80 times per second, which also allows them to fly up to 60 miles per hour (100 km/h). While flying, their heart may beat up to 1,250 times per minute. To keep their little engines going, hummingbirds eat a high-sugar diet of flower nectar. They also eat insects, and sometimes they steal these from spider webs as well as eating the spiders themselves. However, hummingbirds must be careful: they are so small that they sometimes get trapped in the spider webs and die.

WHITE IBIS

LATIN NAME	*Eudocinus albus*
LENGTH	25" (64 cm)
WINGSPAN	38" (97 cm)
WEIGHT	2 lb (900 g)
DIET	Crustaceans and insects
RANGE	Southeastern U.S. to northern South America
NESTING SITE	In trees or shrubs, sometimes on the ground

I IBIS

The long curved beak of the White Ibis helps it catch aquatic insects, shrimp, crabs, fish and other small water animals. As it wades through marshes or mudflats, it finds food by probing its beak into the mud or sweeping it back and forth in the water. When it is feeding, the ibis may have "attendants." These are other species of birds that stick close to the feeding ibis and catch prey that is scared out into the open by the ibis's beak. When egrets, Little Blue Herons and Willets (a large shorebird) hunt beside an ibis, they catch more prey than when they hunt by themselves. This usually doesn't hurt the ibis's feeding because the prey that the other birds catch has already gone beyond the ibis' beak. However, sometimes a Willet will actually steal prey right from the ibis, so this team doesn't always work well — at least for the ibis.

Juvenile White Ibis

J JAY

You'll often hear a jay before you see one. In fact, you will usually hear more than one because they tend to travel in groups. Jays are part of the crow family and, like crows, are quite intelligent. They have a lot of different calls that mean different things. For example, the Blue Jay has a squeaky "wheedelee" call that it uses during courtship. Another call is the "jay" call. When this call is given softly it means "everyone come over here," but when given loudly means "there is a predator over here, come and help me scream at it so it leaves us alone!" Calling loudly at a predator is known as "mobbing," and jays, chickadees, crows and many other birds do it. If you learn the mobbing calls of small birds, you can follow them and try to see what they are yelling at. This often turns out to be a hawk or an owl, but sometimes the small birds make a mistake. I once found a flock of 40 Blue Jays all screaming at a harmless and quite confused porcupine!

BLUE JAY

LATIN NAME	Cyanocitta cristata
LENGTH	11" (28 cm)
WINGSPAN	16" (41 cm)
WEIGHT	3 oz (85 g)
DIET	Insects, nuts, acorns, fruits, seeds; some carrion, small mammals, birds and eggs
RANGE	Eastern North America
NESTING SITE	One to over 98 ft (30 m) in a tree

Green Jay

K KINGFISHER

Kingfishers are found all over the world except for the Arctic and Antarctic. While there are about 95 different species of kingfishers, only one is found in most of North America. The Belted Kingfisher looks a bit like a stubby Blue Jay with a huge beak. This beak is its fishing tool. The Belted Kingfisher perches on a branch or hovers over water until it sees a suitably sized fish below. It then dives down, sometimes totally immersing itself in an attempt to catch its prey. Belted Kingfishers eat mostly fish, but they also are known to catch crayfish, insects, frogs and even small mammals. Once their dinner is caught, they fly to a branch and bash their meal against their perch until it is stunned. Then they swallow their prey whole.

BELTED KINGFISHER

LATIN NAME	*Megaceryle alcyon*
LENGTH	13" (33 cm)
WINGSPAN	20" (51 cm)
WEIGHT	5 oz (150 g)
DIET	Fish, some crayfish, insects and other small animals
RANGE	Most of North America
NESTING SITE	A burrow is dug into a river bank; sometimes in a gravel pit, sand pile or ditch

L

LOON

Loon: an unmajestic name for a very majestic bird. The loon gets its name from a distress call it makes that sounds like maniacal or loony laughter. This call is one of the distinctive sounds of the northern wilderness. If you practice, you can actually speak "loon." By either making the sound in your throat or learning how to blow through your cupped hands, you can make a loon think you are a loon, too. Try this on a lake where a loon is fishing and you might be able to get it to swim over and check you out! If the loon is with its chicks, though, it might not respond by getting closer. Loon parents may protect their young by diving and surfacing farther away. Then they call and dive again. This is thought to be a distraction display to lead predators away. Once the danger has passed, the loon parents will return to their young. They usually have two chicks and, as you can see, when the chicks are tired, they get to hitch a ride.

COMMON LOON

LATIN NAME	*Gavia immer*
LENGTH	32" (81 cm)
WINGSPAN	54" (137 cm)
WEIGHT	9 lb (4.1 kg)
DIET	Mostly fish; some invertebrates such as crayfish and leeches
RANGE	Most of Canada, Alaska and the northern U.S. as well as most of the west and east coasts of North America; also Greenland, Iceland and Scotland
NESTING SITE	On shoreline, muskrat house or floating mat of vegetation

MEADOWLARK

Look at the photos of the Western Meadowlark and the Eastern Meadowlark. Can you see a difference? These two species look almost identical to one another, each seeming to wear a yellow V-necked sweater. So how do you tell them apart? The easiest way is by listening. The Eastern Meadowlark has a very high-pitched whistled song that sounds a bit like, "Sweet spring is here!" On the other hand, the Western Meadowlark's song is a jumble of very flutelike notes that have a much more musical quality to them than the Eastern Meadowlark's song. These songs not only help us tell the birds apart, they help the meadowlarks tell each other apart, too. By singing different songs, each male will be able to tell other males of their own species to stay away from their territory. As well, each male will only attract a mate of its own species. Once they find a mate, the nesting cycle can begin. Finding a meadowlark nest is very challenging because, even though it is on the ground, it is well hidden in long grass and often has a grassy roof.

Eastern Meadowlark

WESTERN MEADOWLARK

LATIN NAME	*Sturnella neglecta*
LENGTH	9.5" (24 cm)
WINGSPAN	14.5" (37 cm)
WEIGHT	3.4 oz (97 g)
DIET	Seeds and insects
RANGE	Central and western North America
NESTING SITE	On the ground in dense vegetation

NIGHTHAWK

The Common Nighthawk is a master of blending in with its environment. Its feathers are mottled with grays and browns to help it blend in to its environment. When it is perched, it closes its eyes and looks just like a broken branch or a bit of tree bark. To enhance this look, it usually perches parallel to the branch instead of perpendicular or crosswise to it like most other birds. The nighthawk needs to be camouflaged because it usually only hunts in the evening and early morning, so it needs to stay hidden from predators during the day. The nighthawk's camouflage abilities don't stop at its plumage, either. These birds nest on the ground, but they don't build a nest to hide their eggs. Instead, their eggs look like a couple of round stones. Even their downy young blend in with the ground. Hiding is a family affair for nighthawks.

Common Nighthawk nest

COMMON NIGHTHAWK

LATIN NAME	*Chrodeiles minor*
LENGTH	9.5" (24 cm)
WINGSPAN	24" (61 cm)
WEIGHT	2.2 oz (62 g)
DIET	Flying insects
RANGE	Much of Canada south to central South America
NESTING SITE	On the ground or on gravel-covered roof tops

O

OWL

Owls are some of the best known birds, even though most people have never seen one. Most are nocturnal and have special adaptations for getting around in the dark. Their eyes are huge and this allows them to gather more light than other birds. Because their eyes are so big, owls don't have any room for muscles to move their eyes back and forth or up and down in their sockets. So, owls always stare straight ahead and must swivel their heads to see around them. Owls also have incredible hearing. This allows them to catch food even when it is very dark out. The Barn Owl can hear so well that even when a scientist put one in a room with no light, it could still catch a mouse by only hearing it move. The Great Gray Owl can pinpoint the sound of a mouse under up to 18 inches (45 cm) of snow and then plunge through the snow to catch its hidden prey!

Barn Owl

GREAT GRAY OWL

LATIN NAME	*Strix nebulosa*
LENGTH	27" (68 cm)
WINGSPAN	52" (132 cm)
WEIGHT	2.4 lb (1100 g)
DIET	Mostly voles, shrews and pocket gophers; some rabbits, squirrels and birds
RANGE	Alaska, central and western Canada, northern and western United States, northern Europe and Asia
NESTING SITE	Old raptor and crow nests, tops of broken tree trunks

Brown Pelican

P PELICAN

A wonderful bird is the pelican,
His bill will hold more than his belican!

So wrote Dixon Lanier Merritt in 1910. And how right he was. The large American White Pelican's beak pouch can hold approximately 3 gallons (12 liters) of water, and that's much more than its stomach could handle. The pelican uses its interesting beak as a net to catch fish, straining the water out of the edges before swallowing its catch. A group of American White Pelicans may work as a team, herding fish into shallow water and then plunging their open beaks under the surface all at the same time to scoop the concentrated fish. The smaller Brown Pelican can fly above the waves and then dive into the water to fill its pouch. Pelicans are large waterbirds and so they need to eat quite a lot. The American White Pelican eats approximately 4 pounds (1.8 kg) of fish per day. This pelican has one of the biggest wingspans of any North American bird — up to 9.5 feet (2.9 meters)!

WHITE PELICAN

LATIN NAME	*Pelecanus erythrorhynchos*
LENGTH	62" (157 cm)
WINGSPAN	108" (274 cm)
WEIGHT	16.5 lb (7.5 kg)
DIET	Fish; sometimes amphibians and crayfish
RANGE	Central North America to Central America
NESTING SITE	On the ground, often on an island

QUAIL

Quail are small chickenlike birds that are often seen running around in small groups. The Gambel's Quail is found in the southwestern United States. It has beautiful plumage, including a group of about six feathers that make the nifty plume that sticks out from its forehead. This and other parts of the male's plumage are shown off during a mating display. During this display, the male tries to attract a mate by bowing up and down, flashing his chestnut cap and the dark and light patches on his belly, as well as making his head plume vibrate. He may also offer the female some bits of food. Scientists studying these display behaviors have found that the females are attracted to males that offer the most food, not the ones with the nicest feathers.

Female Gambel's Quail

GAMBEL'S QUAIL

LATIN NAME	*Callipepla gambelii*
LENGTH	10" (25 cm)
WINGSPAN	14" (36 cm)
WEIGHT	6 oz (180 g)
DIET	Seeds, leaves, fruits and insects
RANGE	Southwestern U.S. and northwest Mexico
NESTING SITE	Usually on the ground under a shrub or cactus

R RAVEN

One of the coolest things I've ever seen a bird do was done by a Common Raven. While I was leading a group on a nature hike, a raven started flying toward us. It was only a few feet above us when it turned over and flew upside down! It did this for a few flaps and then turned right-side up and continued on its way. Ravens are incredibly intelligent and are often called the Trickster by many Native peoples. They have been known to hitch rides in the backs of open pickup trucks and to fly overhead and drop frozen dog poop on people below. A pair of ravens was seen stealing dog food by having one raven distract the dog while the other ate its kibble. Then the ravens would trade places. In light of all these tricks, I figure that the raven we saw fly upside down did it to show off ... and because it knew that we would be jealous.

COMMON RAVEN

LATIN NAME	*Corvus corax*
LENGTH	24" (61 cm)
WINGSPAN	53" (135 cm)
WEIGHT	2.6 lb (1.2 kg)
DIET	Carrion, small animals, insects, eggs, seeds, fruit and garbage
RANGE	Arctic Canada to Central America; also Greenland, Iceland, Europe, Asia and northern Africa
NESTING SITE	Cliffs, trees, towers, silos, bridges and buildings, usually 15–65 ft (4.5–20 m) up

SKIMMER

The winner of the weirdest beak award goes to the skimmer. This member of the gull and tern family has a lower mandible (the lower half of its beak) that is longer than the upper mandible. It hunts by skimming the surface of the water with its lower mandible slicing through the water. Once its lower mandible touches a fish it clamps down on it. The skimmer even has special pupils that are vertical, like a cat's. This may cut down on the glare of the sun reflecting on the water. However, they don't just hunt during the day. Sometimes they can be seen skimming in the evening or at night. They can do this because they are hunting by touch instead of looking for the fish. When they aren't feeding, you can sometimes see them resting on beaches in large flocks.

BLACK SKIMMER

LATIN NAME	*Rynchops niger*
LENGTH	18" (46 cm)
WINGSPAN	44" (112 cm)
WEIGHT	11 oz (300 g)
DIET	Fish
RANGE	East coast of North America and Central America, coasts and large rivers of northern South America
NESTING SITE	Beaches, sand bars, coastal marshes and flat top roofs

LATIN NAME	*Piranga olivacea*
LENGTH	7" (18 cm)
WINGSPAN	11.5" (29 cm)
WEIGHT	1 oz (28 g)
DIET	Insects, spiders and fruit
RANGE	Southeastern Canada and northeastern U.S., Panama to northern South America
NESTING SITE	In a tree usually 7–65 ft (2–20 m) up

Golden-naped Tanager

TANAGER

The male Scarlet Tanager is so red that it seems to almost shine. In one of his courtship displays, he will perch below a female and droop his wings to show off his bright red back. There are four tanager species that are regularly found in North America north of Mexico. All four are known as Neotropical migrants. This means that they migrate south into Central and South America for the winter. Like most other small Neotropical migrants, they do most of their migrating at night. These birds can use stars and the Earth's magnetic force to navigate in the dark. There are likely other navigational techniques they use that we haven't discovered yet. When the North American tanagers reach Central and South America, they join over 200 other species of tanagers. These birds seem to come in every color combination and pattern imaginable, making the tanager family one of the most beautiful in the world.

U UPLAND SANDPIPER

When is a sandpiper not a sandpiper? Well, the Upland Sandpiper doesn't usually spend any time on sandy beaches or muddy lake edges like many of its relatives. Instead, it would prefer to hang out in a grassy field and sit on an old fence post. The Upland Sandpiper is a grassland species and is found across central North America as well as Alaska and the Yukon. It builds its nest on the ground among tall grasses and small shrubs. Like many other ground nesters, it has a special way of protecting its eggs and flightless chicks. When a predator approaches, the sandpiper does a distraction display. It pretends to have a wing injury and drags itself along the ground while calling. This is to try and lead the predator away from the eggs or nestlings. When the sandpiper has led the danger far enough away, it just takes off, leaving the fooled predator behind.

UPLAND SANDPIPER

LATIN NAME	*Bartramia longicauda*
LENGTH	12" (30 cm)
WINGSPAN	26" (66 cm)
WEIGHT	6 oz (170 g)
DIET	Mostly invertebrates, some seeds
RANGE	Alaska, central North America and Brazil to central Argentina
NESTING SITE	On the ground in vegetation

TURKEY VULTURE

LATIN NAME	*Cathartes aura*
LENGTH	26" (66 cm)
WINGSPAN	67" (170 cm)
WEIGHT	4 lb (1830 g)
DIET	Mostly carrion
RANGE	Southern Canada to southern tip of South America
NESTING SITE	Caves, cliff ledges, mammal burrows, fallen hollow trees, stumps, abandoned buildings

V VULTURE

While it may not win a beauty contest, the vulture still gets the prize for cleanliness. Most vultures eat carrion and that cleans up the environment. Their bald or mostly unfeathered heads allows them to dig deep into the carcass for the best bits without getting too messed up. They have very strong and sharp beaks, which help them tear pieces off. Most vultures find their food by soaring high in the sky and watching with their keen eyes. The Turkey Vulture, however, has a special way to find its food. It can actually smell a rotting carcass from quite a distance and can find it without seeing it first. Its beak is designed to allow a lot of air to flow past its nostrils so it can detect even the slightest smell of death. This allows Turkey Vultures to find food in forests where seeing it from above is impossible because of tree leaves. Natural gas companies use this amazing adaptation to help them find leaks in their pipelines. They put a rotting carcass smell into the pipeline and can tell where the leaks are by watching Turkey Vultures gather over parts of the pipe!

Lappet-faced Vulture

Pileated Woodpecker

W WOODPECKER

How does a woodpecker smash its beak into the side of a tree and not get a headache? These tough birds have a special cushioning system inside their skulls that stops their brains from becoming bruised. Woodpeckers use their incredible woodpecking talent for many purposes. One is to get food. Most woodpeckers eat insects and many of these can be found inside wood. These insects are protected from most birds because the birds can't get them through the bark and wood, but woodpeckers can. Acorn Woodpeckers also like to eat, you guessed it, acorns. They store extra acorns by drilling small holes into tree trunks and then pounding acorns into them. These acorns are in so tight that other animals have trouble stealing them. Another use of pecking is for communication. Woodpeckers that drum loudly on a tree can proclaim their territory and attract mates. Last, but not least, woodpeckers can drill a cavity into a tree and use it as a nest. Most woodpeckers do not reuse last year's cavity, so this leaves it open to new tenants such as bluebirds, chickadees, wrens, flying squirrels and mice. Pileated Woodpeckers are crow-sized woodpeckers that make themselves such big nests that they end up providing homes for large birds such as owls, kestrels and even Wood Ducks.

ACORN WOODPECKER

LATIN NAME	*Melanerpes formicivorus*
LENGTH	9" (23 cm)
WINGSPAN	17.5" (44 cm)
WEIGHT	2.8 oz (79 g)
DIET	Mostly acorns and some insects, seeds, fruit and sap
RANGE	Western U.S. to Mexico
NESTING SITE	Drills cavities in dead limbs of mature trees

XANTUS'S MURRELET	
LATIN NAME	*Synthliboramphus hypoleucus*
LENGTH	10" (25 cm)
WINGSPAN	15" (38 cm)
WEIGHT	6 oz (170 g)
DIET	Mostly fish, some crustaceans
RANGE	West coast of southern British Columbia to Baja California, Mexico
NESTING SITE	Caves and crevices in cliffs

XANTUS'S MURRELET

The Xantus's Murrelet is a small seabird that is in the same family as its famous cousin, the Atlantic Puffin. A female Xantus's Murrelet performs quite a feat during the breeding season. She may weigh only 6 ounces (168 g) but she lays an egg that is 1.3 ounces (37 g). That's approximately 22 percent of her body weight! This is one of the biggest eggs in relation to the adult's body size of any bird in the world. And then, about eight days later, she lays another one! The resulting chicks that hatch from these eggs are quite large and have feet almost as big as their parents. This is a good thing because when they are only one to two days old, they have to make an incredible journey. They crawl from their burrow nests and make their way to the sea to find their parents. This journey may include having to jump off a cliff and fall over 200 feet (60 m)!

Y YELLOWLEGS

Yellowlegs are sandpipers like the Upland Sandpiper, but unlike their grassland cousin, they like to wade around in water to look for food. In fact, they are quite good at using all kinds of different aquatic habitats. They normally breed in the boreal forests of North America, choosing wet muskeg bogs as nesting sites. In this area, the yellowlegs are known to perch in trees, which seems odd for a shorebird. Sometimes they breed in the subarctic tundra. During migration and in the winter, the yellowlegs hang out on the edges of lakes, ponds, slow rivers, swamps, meadows, flooded fields, coastal marshes, mangroves and sandbars. They don't seem to be too picky! There are two yellowlegs species. The largest is called the Greater Yellowlegs, and the smallest is the Lesser Yellowlegs. Both have bright yellow legs and so they can be hard to tell apart at first. Look at the photos: you might notice that the Greater Yellowlegs has a longer beak and looks a bit bulkier than the Lesser Yellowlegs.

Lesser Yellowlegs

GREATER YELLOWLEGS

LATIN NAME	*Tringa melanoleuca*
LENGTH	14" (36 cm)
WINGSPAN	28" (71 cm)
WEIGHT	6 oz (160 g)
DIET	Usually invertebrates and small fish
RANGE	Southwestern Alaska, the northern parts of the Canadian provinces, the east and west coasts of North America, the extreme southern U.S., Mexico to South America
NESTING SITE	On the ground under coniferous trees

ZONE-TAILED HAWK

The Zone-tailed Hawk may use a special strategy called mimicry to sneak up on its prey. Most animals learn that the carrion-eating Turkey Vulture won't harm them. The Zone-tailed Hawk may take advantage of this trust by pretending to be a Turkey Vulture. It has similarly colored wings and flies with its wings tilted upward, rocking back and forth in the air like a Turkey Vulture. Potential prey may not take notice of the vulturelike hawk getting closer and closer until it is too late. When the hawk gets close enough, it will dive toward its prey using bushes, trees or rocks to conceal its approach until it can make a grab. The Zone-tailed Hawk eats a wide variety of prey including ground squirrels, chipmunks, rabbits, quail, woodpeckers, sparrows, robins, lizards and snakes.

ZONE-TAILED HAWK

LATIN NAME	*Buteo albonotatus*
LENGTH	20" (51 cm)
WINGSPAN	51" (130 cm)
WEIGHT	1.8 lb (810 g)
DIET	Birds, small mammals and reptiles
RANGE	Southwestern U.S. to northern Bolivia
NESTING SITE	On cliffs or in trees

GLOSSARY

aerial – Something that is done in the air.

animal – Any living thing that is not a plant, fungus, bacteria or other one-celled organism. For example, birds, insects and spiders are all animals. "Animal" is often confused with "mammal." A mammal is an animal that usually has hair or fur and the female produces milk for its young. Mice, whales, bats, elephants and humans are all mammals.

behavior – How a bird conducts itself in a certain situation.

call – A noise or sound made by a bird that is not usually linked to attracting a mate or defending a territory. Contact calls are used to keep birds in a flock together. Alarm or distress calls are used to announce the presence of a potential predator.

camouflage – The coloring and pattern of a bird that allows it to blend in with its surroundings so it stays hidden.

courtship display – *See* mating display.

distraction display – When a bird pretends to be injured to lure a potential predator away from the bird's nest or young.

feeding strategy – A certain process that a bird uses to get food.

female – The "woman" bird.

hover – To stay in one place in the air.

male – The "man" bird.

mate – A bird's partner with whom it creates eggs.

mating display – A set of actions or postures that a bird uses to attract a mate. For example, a peacock spreading out its tail feathers.

mimicry – When a bird pretends to be and/or looks like something else to protect itself or provide food for itself.

naturalist – Someone who observes and studies nature.

nest – The place where a bird lays its eggs. Note: Most birds do not use a nest when they are not taking care of eggs or young birds.

nesting cycle – The sequence of a bird building a nest, laying eggs, sitting on the eggs and caring for the young birds when they hatch.

nesting site – The place where a bird builds its nest and/or lays its eggs. Note: Some birds do not build a nest, but lay their eggs directly on the bare ground, in a tree cavity or in the old nest of another bird.

nocturnal – Active at night.

perch (noun) – A branch or other elevated spot that a bird can rest on.

perch (verb) – To rest or settle.

plumage – A bird's feathers.

prey – Live animals that carnivorous birds eat.

raptor – A bird that usually catches other animals for its food. Also known as a bird of prey. A term most often used for hawks, eagles, falcons and owls.

rare – A bird that is uncommon or seldom seen.

song – A usually complex and sometimes musical sound made by a bird that is trying to attract a mate and/or defend a territory.

species – A kind or sort of living creature. For example, a Peregrine Falcon is a species falcon. A Merlin is another species of falcon. A Common Goldeneye is a species of duck. A species of animal usually only mates with another of the same species.

store – Hide food that can later be found again and eaten.

talons – The claws on the end of bird toes. A term usually used for the claws of raptors.

territory – The area or home range that a bird needs to find enough food and shelter for itself. If it is the breeding season, this area must be big enough for itself, its mate and its dependent young.